TORNADOES

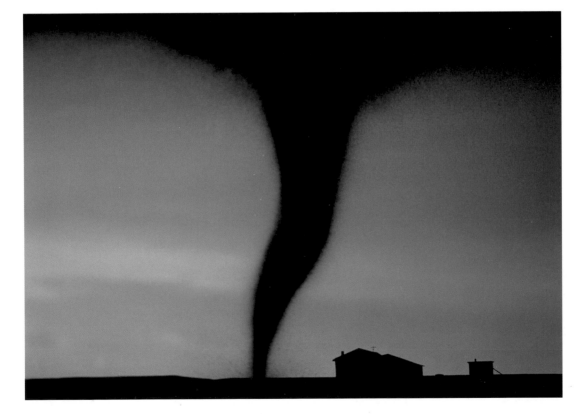

Edited by Colin Baxter Photography
Designed by Colin Baxter Photography
Printed in China

02 03 04 05 5 4 3 2
Library of Congress Cataloging-in-Publication Data available
ISBN 0-89658-522-0

Distributed in Canada by Raincoast Books, 9050 Shaughnessy Street, Vancouver, B.C. V6P 6E5
Published by Voyageur Press, Inc.
123 North Second Street, P.O. Box 338, Stillwater, MN 55082 U.S.A.
651-430-2210, fax 651-430-2211
books@voyageurpress.com
www.voyageurpress.com

Educators, fundraisers, premium and gift buyers, publicists, and marketing managers:
Looking for creative products and new sales ideas? Voyageur Press books are available at special
discounts when purchased in quantities, and special editions can be created to your specifications.
For details contact the marketing department at 800-888-9653.

Photographs copyright © 2001 by

Front Cover © Alan R Moller / Tony Stone
Back Cover © Warren Faidley / Oxford Scientific Films
Page 1 © Warren Faidley / Oxford Scientific Films
Page 4 © Charles Doswell III / Tony Stone Images
Page 6 © Warren Faidley / Oxford Scientific Films
Page 7 © Alan R Moller
Page 9 © Warren Faidley / Oxford Scientific Films
Page 10 © NASA / Science Photo Library
Page 14 © Martin Lisius / Prairie Pictures
Page 15 © Warren Faidley / Oxford Scientific Films
Page 16 © Warren Faidley / Oxford Scientific Films
Page 18 © Roger Hill
Page 19 © Alan R Moller
Page 22 © David Parker / Science Photo Library
Page 24 © Warren Faidley / Oxford Scientific Films
Page 25 © Warren Faidley / Oxford Scientific Films
Page 27 © Alan R Moller / Tony Stone
Page 28 © NASA / Science Photo Library
Page 30 © Warren Faidley / Oxford Scientific Films
Page 33 © Martin Lisius / Prairie Pictures
Page 34 © Hank Baker
Page 37 © Ken Graham / Tony Stone Images

Page 38 © Alan R Moller
Page 39 © Alan R Moller / Tony Stone Images
Page 40 © Alan R Moller
Page 42 © Warren Faidley / Oxford Scientific Films
Page 45 © John Elk / Tony Stone Images.
Page 46 © Timothy Marshall / Tony Stone Images
Page 47 © Alan R Moller / Tony Stone Images
Page 49 © Warren Faidley / Oxford Scientific Films
Page 50 © Alan R Moller / Tony Stone Images
Page 52A © Winston Fraser
Page 52B © Winston Fraser
Page 52C © Hank Baker
Page 52D © Hank Baker
Page 55 © E R Degginger / Science Photo Library
Page 60 © Bruce Coleman Inc. 1112593020
Page 63 © Charles Doswell III / Tony Stone Images
Page 65 © E R Degginger / Science Photo Library
Page 66 © G & H Denzau / BBC Natural History Unit
Page 69 © Bengt Lundberg / BBC Natural History Unit
Page 70 © Paul and Lindamarie Ambrose / Telegraph Colour
Library

Front Cover Photograph: Tornado, Texas, USA.
Page 1: Tornado at dusk.
Page 4: Tornado, near Hodges, Texas.
Page 70: Tornado at sunset.
Back Cover Photograph: Tornado, Midwest, USA.

TORNADOES

H. Michael Mogil

WORLDLIFE
LIBRARY

Voyageur Press

Contents

Introduction

When you hear the word 'tornado' you often imagine scenes of incredible devastation. Sometimes it is a mobile home park that is destroyed; at other times a large part of an entire town or small city. Even though tornadoes are relatively small (nearly all are less than a mile across), they often bring winds above 100 mph (160 kmph), and occasionally some that exceed the 300 mph (480 kmph) barrier.

The term tornado is derived from the Spanish word *tornar* or its Latin equivalent *tornare* (to turn) and the Spanish word *tronada* (thunderstorm). As such, a tornado is defined by the National Weather Service (NWS) as a 'violently rotating column of air in contact with the ground.' Tornadoes come in all sizes, shapes, and colors. Some look like a typical 'elephant trunk,' while others look and move more like snakes. Some may be a true condensation funnel (which we see as a rotating, cloud-like, grayish appendage

Thunderstorm with cloud-to-ground lightning and precipitation.

coming from the storm); others are actually clouds of dirt, dust or water spray. Sometimes, the tornado may even be invisible, except for a funnel cloud high above the ground and a small rotating cloud of dust beneath, near the ground. Although these two may appear to be separate, they are linked. There is nothing in the definition of tornado that says you have to be able to see the rotating column of air!

For the most part, tornadoes last less than ten minutes; however, some (such as the

Unusual, small-based thunderstorm with wall cloud and tornado.

Tri-state tornado of March 1925 and the Mattoon tornado of May 1917) have documented lifetimes of 3 and 7 hours respectively. Because of the way tornado damage has been documented and how our understanding of these storms has changed, many of the longer-lived tornadoes reported before 1950 are believed to have been not just one, but a series of tornadoes.

On some days, just a few tornadoes may develop; at other times, outbreaks of ten or more tornadoes in a certain area may be spawned in a single afternoon or evening. There has been one exceptional tornado event, called the Super Tornado Outbreak. This began on 3 April 1974. In one 24-hour period, spanning two calendar days, some 150 twisters struck the corridor between the Mississippi River and the Appalachian Mountains.

Tornadoes have struck in many places around the world. The United Kingdom, France, Germany, Russia, Bangladesh, Japan, and Australia are among the places that have experienced these storms. We'll look into global tornados later in the book. But most of the information that follows focuses on United States tornadoes simply because this country has the greatest number, and the best documentation of them.

Every state in the US has experienced at least one tornado, although the largest number occur in 'tornado alley,' a loosely described portion of the central Plains which includes Nebraska, Kansas, Oklahoma, and parts of north Texas. Tornadoes occur in all seasons, although peak incidence is in the spring. They can occur at any time of day; yet it is the sun's heating power that drives their peak frequency between about 3 pm and 9 pm local time. Although their photographic beauty is awe-inspiring, their destructive power is legendary. No wonder people are drawn to them – to study, predict, and even to chase them.

In an average year, more than 1000 tornadoes are reported across the United States, resulting in about 80 deaths and over 1500 injuries. The number of reported tornadoes has been more or less steadily increasing since the tornado warning program began in 1951 and storm chasing started in the early 1970s. For details on the evolution of a warning program in the US, visit the National Oceanic and Atmospheric Administration (NOAA) website.

Without its visible dust cloud, this northwest Texas tornado might be called a funnel cloud.

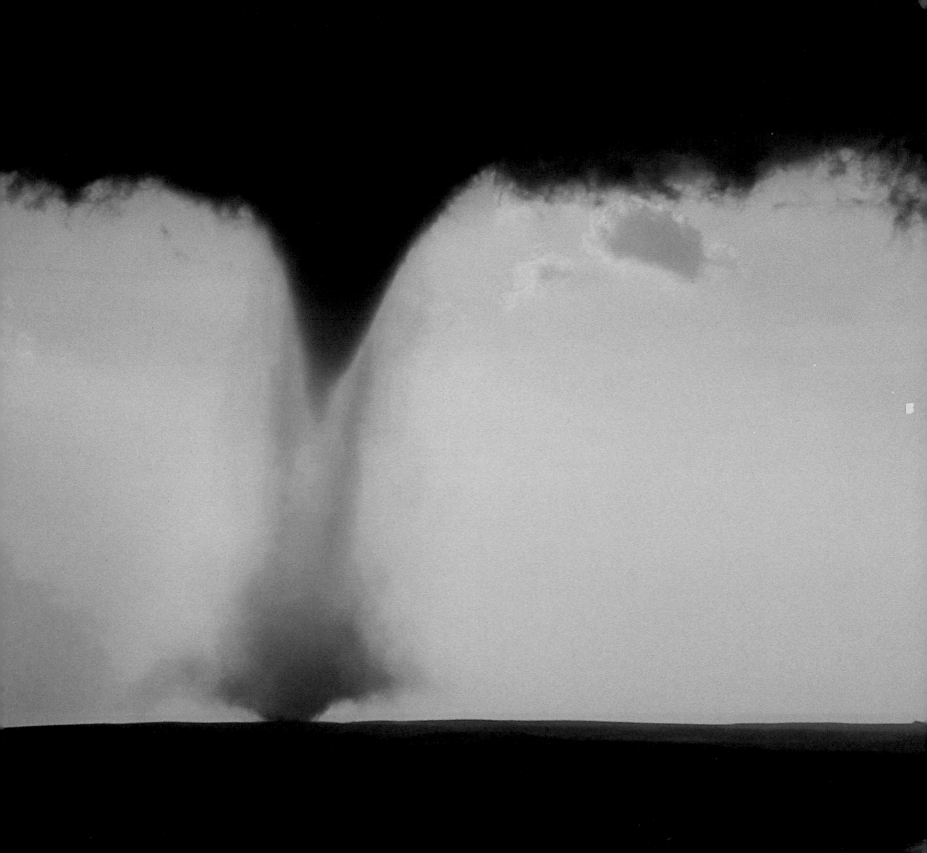

Weather Maps

Hollywood filmmakers have capitalized on our fascination with these vicious storms. Several different tornadoes destroyed the countryside in the 1990s movie *Twister,* and it took only one giant tornado to carry Dorothy off to see the Wizard of Oz in the 1939 classic. While there was some fact and some fiction presented in each of these films, one has to look for the many swirls and whirls that exist in the world around us to really understand tornadoes. A good place to start is right on your television or newspaper weather report.

The daily weather map you see is filled with a series of H's (high-pressure systems) and L's (low-pressure systems), representing a myriad of clockwise and counterclockwise swirls, respectively. If you are in the Southern hemisphere, the sense of the swirls is reversed due to how the Earth's rotation is described. Lows are often linked together by fronts, which can give them a wave-like pattern. Thanks to the Norwegians in the early part of the twentieth century, meteorologists have used the term 'wave cyclone' to describe the lifecycle of middle latitude low-pressure systems along fronts. The term 'cyclone' actually applies to any low-pressure swirl in the atmosphere.

Satellite images show the swirl pattern, too. They also show a larger-scale series of waves that are comprised of mountain-like ridges that bulge poleward (these are highs) and u-shaped troughs that bulge equatorward (lows). From their position 22,300 miles (35,900 km) above the equator, geostationary weather satellites (which are locked into an orbit that matches the earth's rotation) watch how clouds transform and move across the Earth's surface. The patterns made by the clouds on infrared (heat) and visible (reflected light) imagery typically mark the same waviness seen on weather maps.

There are also polar orbiting weather satellites. These orbit the Earth along a slanted path (much like the space shuttle does) and are much closer to the Earth than their geostationary counterparts. The result is that the orbit period is much faster than Earth's and the Earth actually spins below the satellite's orbit. Polar orbiting satellites see different parts

From the space shuttle Columbia, *the setting sun highlights the anvils of thunderstorms over New Guinea.*

of the Earth each orbit, but what they see is in more detail.

Newer types of satellite images, which are only now starting to be used in a more widespread manner on television, show the wave pattern even better. Called water vapor imagery (because horizontal variations in atmospheric water vapor content are relatively easy to see), this imagery almost shows the fluid flow of air. Although air behaves much like water, air is so much lighter that it flows faster. Due to technological advances, these images, which are really composed of small data sets called pixels or picture elements, can be 'false-color enhanced'. This allows meteorologists to transform an image filled with shades of gray into a colorized image in which important features often 'jump out' at the viewer.

Many television stations (especially The Weather Channel™) show image sequences of satellite imagery called 'loops'. Because the orbit of the geostationary satellite matches the rotation of the Earth, the satellite is fooled into thinking the Earth isn't moving. This allows meteorologists to create time sequences of the images, in which the Earth remains fixed but the clouds change. These are called loops because the sequences recycle or loop over and over.

Another key feature of weather maps is the jet stream. This is a narrow ribbon, which can be both horizontal and vertical, along which winds are blowing faster than in places adjacent to it. This differential motion is the same as a rower's oar makes in the water. It is this wave pattern form that helps to create the weather features we see on weather maps. To the left of the fastest moving air in the jet stream, a counterclockwise or low-pressure system forms; to the right, a clockwise or high-pressure system forms (note: the sense of rotation is exactly opposite in the Southern hemisphere – lows spin clockwise and highs counterclockwise).

Meteorologists call this and other significant changes in wind speed or direction over small distances 'wind shear'. In its worst case, 'wind shear' has been linked as a contributing factor in several major airplane crashes. However, events such as the crash involving a Delta Airlines plane landing at Dallas in 1982 and the near-miss to President Reagan's *Air Force One* at Andrews AFB in Maryland in 1983 involved straight winds associated with thunderstorms, not circular or tornadic winds. The shear comes into play because the wind speed and/or direction can change quickly over either small horizontal and/or vertical distances, as well as quickly in time. This is especially dangerous when airplanes are landing or taking off.

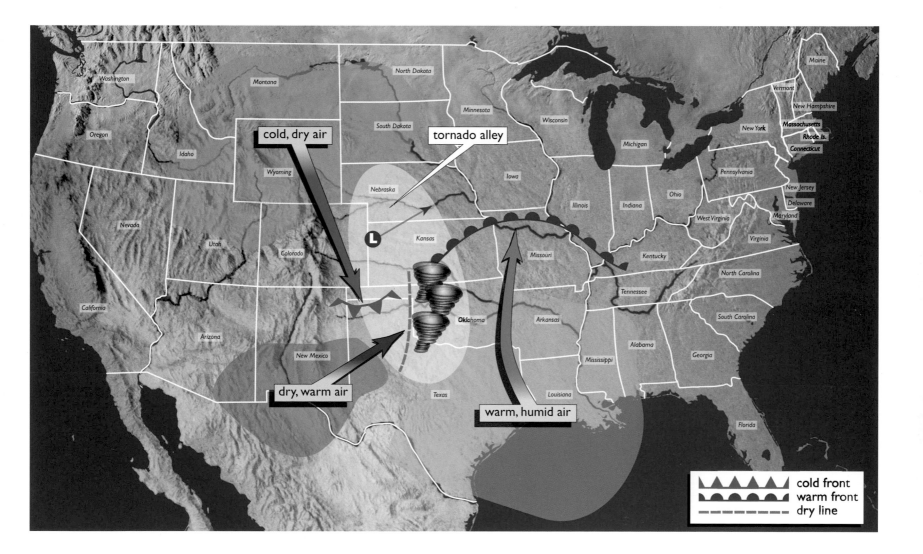

'Tornado Alley' (yellow) is created as low-pressure systems move eastward from the Rockies, and generate the favored breeding ground for tornadic thunderstorms. This involves the clash of cold, dry air from Canada; warm, moist air from the Gulf of Mexico; and warm, dry air from Mexico and New Mexico.

Up to this point, we've looked primarily at large-scale weather patterns. Yet, within the large-scale wave pattern, many smaller-scale swirls exist, as evidenced by water vapor images. To analyze a United States surface (i.e., ground level) weather map in detail, requires a very large number of weather reporting sites. Because of this, meteorologists typically view localized regions comprised of only a few states, such as the area known as tornado alley.

Why do so many tornadoes generally form in tornado alley? The key lies in understanding the different air masses that are seen on the map. An air mass is a large volume of air that has similar temperature and moisture characteristics across it. Each type of air mass forms over a different land or water region and assumes the characteristics of its 'source region.' An air mass that forms over the Gulf of Mexico, for example, would be warm and humid. One that forms over Arizona and northern Mexico would likely be hot and dry. An air mass that forms over central Canada or Alaska would likely be cold and dry.

Classic thunderstorm with underlit anvil at sunset.

The clash of three different air masses isn't an absolute requirement for tornadic thunderstorms to form. However, tornadoes are more likely to form under these conditions. And the central part of the United States is unique when it comes to this weather pattern. There is no other place on Earth where these three air masses collide so consistently on an ongoing basis. Small wonder that the United States now logs upwards of 1000 twisters a year, while reports from other parts of the world combined don't even begin to approach that number.

A severe thunderstorm, with heavy, wind-blown precipitation, marches across the US Midwest.

The Many Faces of Thunderstorms

Thunderstorms, which spawn tornadoes, form under many conditions. The most common is when warm and humid air rises. This can occur when sunlight heats the ground or water, or when air is forced upwards by mountains, sea breezes or fronts. As the air rises, it moves into lower pressure. This is because the weight of the atmosphere above a place decreases (more air is left below) as one goes higher up. As the air rises, it expands, uses up some internal energy, and cools. Eventually, it will reach its condensation level or dew point (where the invisible water vapor in the air reappears as liquid water droplets) and a cloud is born.

Cumulus cloud bases are usually between 3,000 and 7,000 ft (900 and 2100 m) off the ground; they are closer to the ground in more humid locations and higher up where it is drier. The cloud base is often closest to the ground in mid-morning and rises somewhat during the afternoon as surface temperatures rise. Because the condensation level is at about the same altitude across a small region, the cloud bases will appear to be flat (excluding the effect of perspective), even though the tops of the clouds may be rounded. This cloud type is called 'cumulus' which means heaps or mounds.

As the air continues to rise, the clouds bubble upward, with each bubble showing where the updraft of rising air is located. When the cloud tops reach about 15,000 ft (4500 m) the cloud is now referred to as a 'towering cumulus'. If the process continues long enough, the clouds will tower to even greater heights. Eventually, the clouds will reach an altitude where they can no longer keep rising. This is typically between 30,000 and 50,000 ft (9,000 and 15,200 m), but can sometimes reach heights of 60,000 ft (18,300 m). At this level, the air is so cold that the cloud top becomes filled with ice crystals and snow flakes. This gives the top of the cloud a 'fuzzy' appearance, much like a cirrus or cirrostratus cloud. Then, upper level winds start to blow the cloud top horizontally, creating an anvil shape. The cloud, now transformed into a thunderstorm or cumulonimbus cloud, brings thunder, lightning, heavy rain, and sometimes even severe weather like hail, strong winds, and tornadoes.

Even small, high-based Arizona thunderstorms can produce deadly cloud-to-ground lightning.

The life cycle of a typical cumulonimbus cloud includes the growth or updraft stage, described above. But, once rain and snow, and the cold air from the upper portions of the cloud, cut off the updraft, it is replaced with a downdraft. Soon, the cloud rains itself out, leaving behind only cirrus or other 'debris' clouds.

Individual cumulus clouds aren't very large horizontally (most are less than a few miles across). Because they are so small, they generally last much less than an hour. But cumulus usually occur in groups. Thus, as one cumulus cloud ends its life cycle, another cloud is born. To our untrained eyes, we see what appears to be a larger individual cumulus or cumulonimbus cloud lasting for a long time. A cluster of cumulus will consist of clouds at many different lifecycle stages.

This thunderstorm shows the 'boiling' character of cumulus clouds.

From a satellite perspective, it is possible to see the same type of evolution. Although the satellite can't see the bottom of the thunderstorm well, it has a great view of the cloud top. As a result, satellite images document well the bubble-like towers and the development of the anvil. Late afternoon and early morning are the best times for viewing satellite images; the contrast between sunlit and shadowed parts of the thunderstorm makes seeing these features much easier.

Sometimes thunderstorms form in squall lines; these lines of thunderstorms often have gusty or squally straight-line winds. Squall lines, especially when they are more-or-less continuous, do not usually produce tornadoes. This is because so many individual thunderstorms are interacting and competing for the same energy within the warm and humid air mass.

Thunderstorms can also organize in clusters called mesoscale convective complexes (MCC) or mesoscale convective systems (MCS). These types of systems contain many

Many classic 'supercell' features can be seen in this Kansas storm. A large anvil spreads outward from the storm (upper left), while underneath a banded rotating cloud with a rain-free base approaches. It is pitch black to the right because the tallest part of the storm cloud and heavy rain are blocking the sun.

thunderstorms in various stages of their lifecycle. As a result of this, the MCC or MCS lasts much longer than an individual thunderstorm. These types of systems can move very slowly, producing torrential rains and flooding, or they can race across several states at 50 mph (80 kmph) or more. Some non-tropical MCS systems, called derechoes (pronounced *day-RAY-chos*), have produced strong straight-line surface winds for a period greater than 6 hours over tracks several hundreds of miles long and more than 100 miles (160 km) across. These are usually the result of many shorter-lived thunderstorms collectively producing downburst clusters or families.

Any thunderstorm, but most likely a squall line or MCC / MCS, is capable of producing damaging straight line winds. The resulting damage pattern is often a star-burst (radiating from a certain area) or elongated (with most damage showing a consistent direction matching the movement of the thunderstorms). This is different from tornado damage which is much more scattered.

In the MCS or MCC, as well as in a squall line event, the colder air flowing out of the thunderstorm may cause it to dissipate. But as is often the case in nature, death begets new life. In this case, the cold outflow acts like a miniature cold front and starts lifting the warmer air ahead of the dying thunderstorm, generating a new thunderstorm. If the process continues long enough, a series of thunderstorms results.

While MCSs and MCCs can spawn tornadoes, a more isolated type of thunderstorm, if in a favorable environment, stands a much better chance of doing so. Although there are many varieties of this type of storm, the classic 'supercell' is the one most forecasters have learned to respect. Supercells are large, long-lived storms that can produce a large variety of severe weather. Although the United States is most well-known for these storms, the initial discovery and research into supercell type storms was done in the United Kingdom.

Once a cumulonimbus cloud has formed, it becomes important to determine whether or not the thunderstorm cloud itself is swirling or rotating. If it is, then it becomes a swirl inside a larger swirl (the low-pressure system) and itself can have smaller swirls within it. The largest of these smaller swirls is often referred to as a mesocyclone. Mesocyclones, in turn, are what give birth to tornadoes.

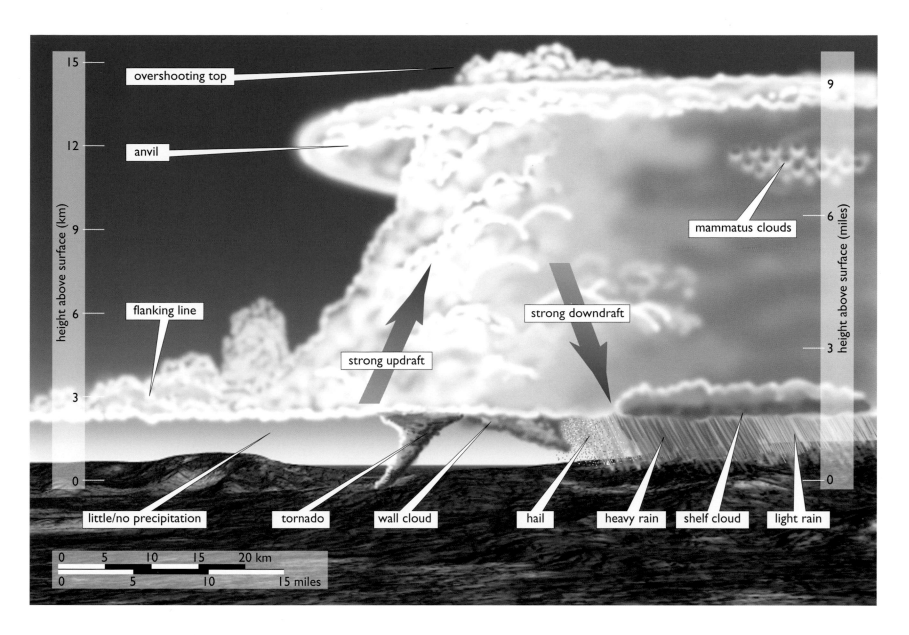

Most 'supercells' look like this. Typically there is a rain-free base that marks the updraft, a precipitation area that shows the downdraft, and features like a shelf cloud and wall cloud that indicate inflow and outflow areas at the base of the storm. This view is looking toward the northwest.

A thunderstorm acts much like a chimney; there is air flowing in at the bottom and exhausting at the top. The faster that air is exhausted at the top, the faster air can flow in at the bottom. This process increases the speed of the air moving upward in the thunderstorm (i.e., its updraft). Exhaust at the top of the thunderstorm is often enhanced by the presence of a nearby jet stream and/or the divergence or spreading apart of winds at the top of the storm. The storm, if strong enough, can even enhance its own divergence at its top.

The pressure near the ground is related to the amount or weight of the air above. If the air is being rapidly exhausted from the top of a thunderstorm, a small-scale low or mesocyclone can develop beneath the exhaust region. This is usually located near to the updraft and at the upwind side of the storm. If air at the top of the storm is moving from the southwest to the northeast, this mesocyclone will be found toward the southwest edge of the thunderstorm.

As a result of these effects, supercell thunderstorms often look like the schematic shown on page 21. In fact, photographs and descriptions of storms that produced tornadoes often show many of the same features shown here.

The lowered cloud base from which the tornado extends is often referred to as a 'wall cloud.' Most of the anvil cloud is blown downwind while the anvil at the southwest edge of the storm sometimes actually builds back into the upper level southwesterly wind flow, especially if divergence around the top of the storm is strong.

Mammatus clouds (pouches hanging from the underside of the anvil) show that the storm's updraft is bringing more air to the top of the storm than can be evacuated by the horizontal wind alone. As a result, some of the excess air is trying to escape by moving downward. Mammatus are especially impressive when underlit by a setting sun.

Striations and bands along the edge of the storm show the curving or curling updraft, too. And the cloud band along the leading edge (northeast or east side) of the storm signals a region where cold, rain- and hail-cooled air is moving outward from the storm. The 'tail cloud' is the cloud that sometimes extends from the rain- or hail-cooled air back towards the updraft near

Mammatus or pouch-like clouds on the underside of a thunderstorm anvil.

the wall cloud. What the supercell schematic (p 21) shows is a special storm circulation in which the updraft and downdraft are separated. Instead of each competing with each other, as they would in a 'typical' thunderstorm, both can operate symbiotically. The updraft region creates the rain and hail, and the downdraft region lets the chilled air and associated precipitation fall out.

We've now discussed three different types of thunderstorms: (1) the typical thunderstorm; (2) the MCC, MCS and/or derecho; and (3) the tornadic storm. Each storm looks quite different and produces significantly different weather. They are summarized in the table below.

As stated above, a mesocyclone develops only when more air leaves the top of the thunderstorm than comes in to take its place from below. Since pressure measures the weight of air above a place, less air above means

Thunderstorm towers contrast with anvil and striated wall cloud.

Thunderstorm type	Size	Lifetime	Attributes / Weather
TYPICAL	Generally less than 5 miles (8 km) across	One hour or less	all have thunder and lightning possible gusty winds and/or heavy rain; may have small hail
MCS, MCC, DERECHO	Can be 100 miles (160 km) across or more	Hours (sometimes 12 or more)	gusty winds and/or heavy rain likely; hail and tornadoes may also occur
TORNADIC	Generally less than 20 miles (32 km) across	One to three hours	very strong and gusty winds, heavy rain, and large hail likely; tornadoes most likely to occur with this type of storm

Rain or hail falling from thunderstorm clouds often appears as a curtain of streamers.

lower pressure below. This generates a wind flow into the low that tries to fill in the missing air. Now a wind circulation matches the low pressure center.

The cumulus-type clouds that mark a developing or established thunderstorm typically have a flat cloud base. This is where rising air expands and cools to its dew point. But at the mesocyclone, the pressure is lower. This results in the condensation level being at a lower altitude and creates a lowered cloud base in that part of the storm called the 'wall cloud.'

If the wall cloud shows signs of rotation, that means the mesolow circulation is fairly strong and that the storm is better able to 'spin up' a tornado. Storm spotters often look for circular motion in the wall cloud and bands or striations around it which also indicate circular motion.

While spotters look for visual clues, Doppler radar probes the skies for actual rotation in and near the thunderstorm. Regular radar ('radar' stands for radio detection and ranging) data shows reflectivity, which is a measure of how much electromagnetic energy sent by the radar is reflected back by raindrops, snowflakes, and hailstones in the storm. It is much like how a ball thrown against a wall bounces back to the thrower. Radar shows where the rainfall and/or hailfall is greatest; wind circulations in the storm can separate precipitation areas, sometimes creating patterns (e.g., hook echoes) that indicate the presence of a tornado. Radar displays show 'echoes' because the energy bounce back is similar to an echo we might hear.

Doppler radar measures the velocity of the precipitation in the storm toward and away from the radar. It is similar to radar guns used in traffic safety and in sports such as baseball and tennis. Although this information does not show a complete circulation, it shows enough of a partial one for meteorologists to infer mesocyclones and tornado vortex signatures (TVS). Because the radar can't actually see a tornado, meteorologists use the 'wind shear' between nearby or adjacent pixels (typically referred to as 'gates'). If the shear exceeds a certain value, a mesocyclone is probably present; if the shear increases, one is likely looking at a TVS. Although a TVS doesn't guarantee a tornado will form, it is considered a very strong indicator.

This supercell-generated wall cloud is very close to the ground.

The Watch and Warning Program

Severe-weather forecasters at NOAA's National Weather Service (NWS) provide a nationwide United States warning system for thunderstorms and other weather hazards. A similar system is in place in Canada. Due to the short time periods involved, the localized nature of these storms, and the myriad of severe weather hazards that may occur, a very specialized warning system has evolved.

At the Storm Prediction Center (SPC) in Norman, Oklahoma, a staff of severe-weather experts monitors the nation for potential thunderstorms and severe thunderstorms 24 hours a day, every day of the year. They examine weather maps at the surface and at various levels through the troposphere, which is the lower atmospheric layer that extends from the ground to about 10 to 12 miles (16 to 19 km) above the ground. They dissect radiosonde balloon data for vertical wind, temperature and moisture profiles. They match these to known patterns and indices for clues to upcoming weather. They also look at computer models of the atmosphere. These are mathematical simulations of the physical laws which govern how the atmosphere behaves. Due to mathematical constraints, scaling factors, and data limitations, models do not provide complete representations of the atmosphere – but they can still show how weather variables may change over timescales from a few hours to several weeks.

Meteorologists also monitor weather satellite data for signs of the jet stream position and for clues about upper-level divergence of winds. They also look for 'boundaries' where localized low-level wind convergence can occur. These include regions where chilled air from other thunderstorms exists, variations in cloud cover over small areas, and places where temperature and pressure are showing significant changes.

Early each day, and several times throughout the day, these forecasters issue 'outlooks' describing the potential for severe weather for the today and tomorrow forecast periods. These are designed to help local National Weather Services' offices ready themselves, in case the weather takes a turn for the worse.

Space Shuttle view of a large-scale low-pressure system over the southern United States.

When severe-weather forecasters feel there is a potential for severe weather during an upcoming period of about six hours, they will issue a severe weather 'watch'. A watch is usually portrayed as a parallelogram and covers about 20,000 to 25,000 sq miles (52,000 to 65,000 sq km). It means that 'severe weather is possible in and near the watch area'. Depending upon the perceived risk factor, forecasters may issue a severe thunderstorm watch: for large hail – greater than three-quarters of an inch in diameter – damaging winds, and/or winds of more than 57 mph (90 kmph). If there is also a threat of tornadoes, the watch will be classified as a tornado watch.

An infrared satellite image showing thunderstorms.

The watch serves two other functions; it helps to activate spotter networks and it puts the communities in the watched area 'on guard'. Spotters are trained individuals, including police, firemen, emergency services officials, amateur radio operators, and others, who can set themselves up in strategic locations around communities and become the community's weather eyes and ears. They typically relay reports back to the NWS, often to an amateur radio base station located at the NWS office. NWS forecasters may also query the spotters for information about the character and movement of a storm.

Many television and radio stations activate special on-screen displays, such as 'crawls' – in which words walk along the bottom of the screen – 'icons' or the word 'watch' – which may or may not flash, and 'sounds' – special beeps or tones, when a watch is issued. These are designed to catch people's attention, including those who may have hearing or visual impairments.

When storms become severe, the NWS enters a 'warning' mode. Warnings are issued for one or more counties by local NWS offices. A warning means the danger is imminent. Sometimes, it is based on Doppler radar or a spotter indicating severe storm characteristics; at other times, it could be the report of actual severe weather. The warning tells people in the path of the storm who might be affected. There are severe thunderstorm warnings and tornado warnings.

While thunderstorms can produce deadly lightning, lightning is not a storm attribute for which watches or warnings are issued. If rainfall is expected to be excessive, flood or flash flood watches or warnings may be issued independently of any severe weather advisories.

Due to the nature of these small, short-lived storms, warnings are not issued until the danger has become great. Even with technological advances, getting word that a tornado is approaching with a five to ten minute lead time is considered good. For some larger storms, warnings of 20 to 30 minutes are now possible. While technology and storm spotter reports make the official warning system function, it is always a good idea to have your own warning system. We have already discussed the overall cloud pattern structure for the supercell thunderstorm. But what about other tornado-producing storms?

Although any thunderstorm may contain one or more supercell cloud attributes, its cloud structure may be less well-defined. Thus, it is important to pay attention to other aspects of the weather. The following can be dangerous in themselves, as well as telling us about potentially dangerous tornadic weather:

• A funnel cloud, no matter how small, can be a forerunner to a significant tornado. Many funnels are weak and last only a few moments. But their presence does indicate strong updrafts and rotation in the thunderstorm.

• Blowing dust or dust swirls under the storm indicate high winds, possibly with rotation. If these occur beneath or near a funnel cloud, it is likely that the tornado is already on the ground, even if it can't be seen.

• Hail, precipitation in the form of ice balls, or irregularly shaped pieces of ice that fall from thunderstorm clouds, indicate strong updrafts. Hail forms as supercooled water – water can sometimes still be liquid at -40°F (-40°C) – and is carried to high altitude where it then freezes. Successive up and down trips in the thunderstorm, caused by turbulence (and/or the movement of supercooled water past a nearly stationary suspended hailstone high up in the cloud), allows the hail to add layers, increasing its size. The size of the hail is directly related to the strength of the updraft; a strong updraft will keep the hailstone suspended for longer, so it will grow to a larger size. Many large hailstones result from the merging of smaller hailstones. When the hail is heavy enough to overcome the updraft, it falls to the ground.

The terminal velocity of hail is also directly related to its size. A 0.4 in diameter hailstone falls at 20 mph (32 kmph). A hailstone slightly bigger than 3 in (76 mm) in diameter will fall at a terminal velocity of over 105 mph (170 kmph). The largest hailstone ever measured fell in Coffeyville, Kansas in September, 1970: it had a diameter of 5.5 inches (14 cm) and fell at about 125 mph (200 kmph). This speed is comparable to that of the highest-ever recorded updraft, estimated independently by aircraft and Doppler remote sensors.

• Although it is not well understood, many people report seeing a greenish-yellow or greenish-gray cloud coloration prior to a hail occurrence. This may be related to light being scattered or refracted by the hailstones in the cloud.

• During the day, an approaching thunderstorm usually darkens the sky dramatically. The degree of darkness is directly related to how much cloud is between the observer and the sun. Taller or thicker clouds, especially those filled with large amounts of hail or rain, often darken the most. A low sun angle, the presence of other clouds, and mountains or forests which block sunlight can also create darkening effects. The darker it gets during the day as a thunderstorm approaches, the greater the risk of bad weather. In the 1970s, a severe thunderstorm with torrential rains moved into Birmingham, Alabama around 4 pm. It got so dark that street lights automatically turned on.

• There are other unusual cloud features, too. These include overshooting tops on distant thunderstorms, back-sheared anvils, mammatus clouds, shelf clouds, and roll clouds. These all foretell significant thunderstorm activity. At night, the storm's lightning display may help you see cloud features that might otherwise be masked by darkness.

• Finally, and especially at night, listen for the tell-tale sound of a jet plane or train. This sound indicates high-speed wind nearby. You may be familiar with the sound of lower-speed air whistling as it flows by trees and buildings; the pitch of the sound is amplified as it flows past them.

A tornado-producing supercell races across the Texas high plains north of Amarillo.

Tornado Formation and Structure

Up to this point, we've seen the larger-scale conditions under which tornadoes may form. But, how does a thunderstorm transform itself into a tornadic thunderstorm? This phenomenon is still under study by scientists, but the latest research points to wind shear, vorticity, and tilting as key concepts to understand.

Sometimes, wind speed and/or direction changes rapidly with increasing altitude in the atmosphere (i.e. wind shear is present). This is especially true near the ground. The classic tornado conditions include winds that veer (e.g., change direction from southeast near the ground, to southwest about a mile above the ground) and increase with height, and a strong inversion or 'cap'. The 'cap' indicates warm air lying on top of cooler air, which initially helps to prevent thunderstorm formation. However, it allows energy to build up beneath the inversion, much like a lid keeps energy trapped in a teapot or a pressure cooker. When that energy is released, thunderstorm growth is often 'explosive'. The veering winds indicate that warmer air is moving into the region, which will help fuel convection or rising air currents; the increasing winds help to create what meteorologists call vorticity or spin.

The spin in the early stages of a tornado's development is around a horizontal axis, much like a paddle wheel of a riverboat or the water wheel on an old grist mill. In the atmosphere, the differences in wind speed between the top and bottom of a thin layer of air starts the layer spinning. This creates a rotating tube of air (see figure on page 36).

Once a thunderstorm starts to form (and any 'cap' is broken), rising air currents cause the tube to bulge upward. Looking down on the two legs of the upwardly bulging tube, one side of the tube is now spinning in a clockwise (high pressure) direction, the other is spinning in a counterclockwise (low pressure) direction. The former becomes the part of the thunderstorm where a small high-pressure center forms and where rain and hail often occur. The latter helps to create the mesocyclone described earlier. The vorticity around the horizontal has now been tipped or tilted so it is spinning around a vertical axis.

Heavy rain and strong straight-line winds will follow the passage of this multi-level shelf cloud.

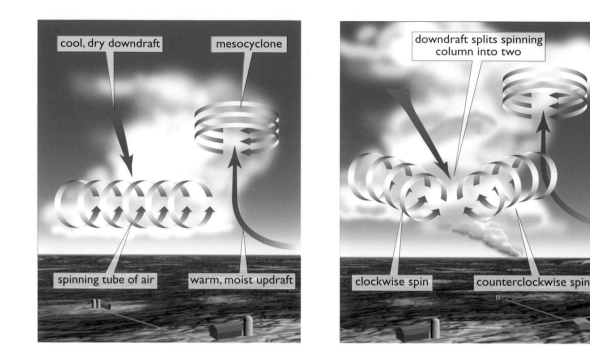

Once the mesocyclone has formed, a cool, often dry downdraft, called a 'rear flank downdraft' pushes down the horizontally spinning tube of air, creating two more vertical spinning tubes. As the counterclockwise spinning tube joins with the mesocyclone and is stretched by the storm's updraft, a tornado is likely to form.

Sometimes a 'rear-flank downdraft' develops on the southwest side of the thunderstorm. Some scientists believe that this chilled air is created as rainfall evaporates while falling through drier air. Here sinking air acts to bend the horizontally-spinning tube downward, creating two additional spins around a vertical axis (see figure on page 36). The counterclockwise spin meets the mesocyclone and is further stretched upward by the rising air currents within the thunderstorm. Much like an ice skater who brings her arms inward while spinning, the rate of spinning increases and a tornado begins.

A large-scale wave cyclone starts out with both warm and cold sectors; eventually cold air surrounds the low, effectively cutting off its energy supply and causing its demise. When this happens, the low is said to have 'occluded.' Sometimes, a new wave forms where the warm, cold, and occluded fronts meet, some distance away from the old low pressure system.

Waterspout over the Java Sea.

The mesocyclone and its associated tornado isn't much different. Warm air feeds into the mesocyclone from the south and southeast; cold air can be found to the northeast in the rain-cooled region and also to the southwest with the 'rear-flank downdraft.' As this rain-cooled air enters the mesocyclone circulation, it acts to occlude it. This helps to increase the spin initially, but also eventually weakens the tornado. In many tornado photographs, it is easy to see the rear flank downdraft wrap around the tornado. The colder, drier air also helps to erode the cloud base, creating a higher cloud base with a lightened area in a curved arch spiraling toward the tornado.

Once formed, the tornado operates much like making a glass of chocolate milk. Add milk and chocolate syrup and then stir. Inside the spin, the fluid level sinks as fluid moves outward (like a centrifuge); this leaves a depression in the center of the spin. Such a pattern is what helps create the 'eye' of a hurricane. It also creates an 'eye' inside the tornado (it's just that we can't see it).

Photographs of waterspouts and some landspouts (which form similarly to waterspouts) show the hollow tube appearance of tornado-like storms. Recent Doppler radar data obtained during storm chases in 1999 in Oklahoma provides similar evidence of an eye-like structure in these storms.

Lots of debris flies around this Texas twister.

If the tornado were to remain stationary, then winds blowing around the storm would represent its only destructive power. But, once the tornado starts to move, the relative effects of the storm's motion must be considered.

Watch as a quarterback on a football team throws a pass. He plants his feet and then moves forward as he throws the ball. The quarterback's forward motion combines with his arm's thrust to increase the ball's forward motion. A quarterback running away from a defensive rush as he throws the ball will produce a subtractive effect and a much weaker forward pass.

This same effect occurs on opposite sides of the rotating tornado. The right front part of the tornado (looking in the direction the tornado is moving) has the additive 'forward motion' effect. The left front part has the subtractive effect as it turns away from the direction of the storm. The faster the storm travels, the greater the difference between the two sides of the tornado.

When the tornado is not exactly in the center of the larger-scale motion driving it (i.e., the wall cloud), the tornado can move around the center point as the entire storm moves. This creates a wobble to the tornado's track (called cycloidal motion) and can produce some erratic damage patterns (see lower figure page 56). Meteorologists found cycloidal pattern marks in a grassy field near Moore, Oklahoma following a tornado on 3 May, 1999. It is interesting to note that NASA scientists have discovered similar cycloidal damage tracks associated with dust devils on Mars.

Tornadoes easily pick up dirt and debris. The bottom half of this
tornado is a cloud of soil. It does a better job of showing the tornado circulation
than the condensation cloud tornado to which it is linked above.

The rising tower of this supercell is completely banded, indicating that the storm itself is rotating. Beneath is a wall cloud and its companion tornado. There are also several areas of precipitation. Some tornadic storms produce so much precipitation that they can hide the tornado from view.

Research and Storm Chasing

Thanks to the video camera, the media and people's general interest in severe storms, storm chasing has become widespread. From its quiet inception with the Union City tornado in 1973, it has grown by leaps and bounds. Today, it's not uncommon for storm chasers to meet and greet each other as they traverse the central and high plains regions of the United States during spring and summer. There are even storm-chase tours available.

But storm chasing is a dangerous business and is best left to the experts. Many storm chasers have reported 'close calls' as storms have suddenly turned or when the chasers have found themselves on unfamiliar roads. From a scientific perspective, storm chasing has provided the basis for much of our current understanding about tornadoes. Some of this is from visual evidence (photographs and videotapes); other aspects result from the testing and use of specialized technology designed to probe these small-scale storms.

Scientists from the US government and from universities, independently and in collaboration, often study particular aspects of the tornado. Some study cloud physics and how raindrops and hailstones interact in a highly turbulent environment; others, changes in atmospheric stability or local changes in surface weather conditions. Still others focus on using Doppler radar to probe the smallest storm features they can possibly detect. To do this, scientists have used instrumented aircraft that are sometimes flown into or near severe thunderstorms, special mobile Doppler radar systems that are driven as close as possible to tornadic storms, and a series of instrumented automobiles that provide a moving mesoscale weather observation network.

In the 1980s, scientists attempted to design and place a tornado-sensing unit in the path of tornadoes. This device, called TOTO (Totable Tornado Observatory) proved unwieldy, unsafe, and unsuccessful and was eventually retired. A variation of this, called Dorothy, became the focus of the movie *Twister*. After tornado chasing and data gathering is done, scientists analyze the data to gain new understandings about tornadoes. Computers are playing an increasing role in this research. There is also work going on in wind engineering (how buildings are damaged and/or destroyed) and in ground and aerial storm-damage surveys. A growing collection of photographs and videotapes is also helping scientists see the many faces of these storms.

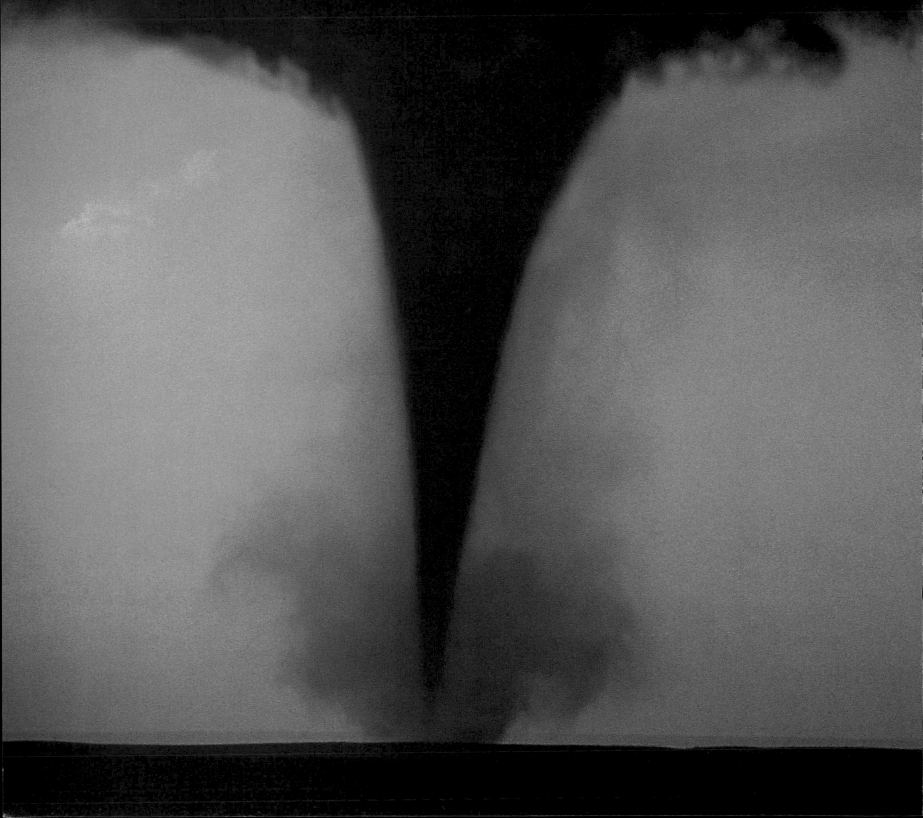

Describing Tornadoes

Tornadoes come in many shapes and sizes. For this reason, severe-weather meteorologists have reviewed their photographic collections and coined terms to describe these different-looking storms. Although the bigger and wider tornadoes may appear to be stronger and more dangerous, there is no absolute relationship between size and strength. In fact, some 'rope' tornadoes which look weaker than much larger ones, actually get more intense as they narrow and tighten, like the spinning effect of an ice skater.

Cone-shaped tornado

If there is a classic image one imagines when hearing the word tornado, this is it. This tornado has a wider top which tapers to a small base. Basically, with a little imagination, it looks like an ice-cream cone.

Rope Tornado

Tornadoes often assume a rope-like, snaky shape in their final minutes; but some can have this shape during their entire lifecycles. Ropes usually indicate that the circulation in the cloud is moving faster than the circulation at the ground; as a result, the tornado gets stretched, eventually separates, and dissipates.

Multiple Vortex Tornado

Many tornadoes contain smaller, rapidly spinning whirls known as sub-vortices, or suction vortices; but they are not always clearly visible. Suction vortices can add over 100 mph (160 kmph) to the relative ground wind in a tornado circulation. As a result, they are often responsible for most cases where narrow arcs of extreme destruction lie next to weak damage within tornado paths. Sub-vortices usually occur in groups of 2 to 5 at once (6 or 7 being uncommon), and usually last less than a minute each. Tornado scientists now believe that most

Classic cone-shaped tornado with large dust cloud near Miami, Texas.

reports of several tornadoes at once, from news accounts and early twentieth-century tornado tales, were actually multiple vortex tornadoes. However, on rare occasions, separate tornadoes can form close to one another as satellite tornadoes.

Satellite Tornado

When a smaller tornado orbits a larger one, it is referred to as a satellite tornado. A satellite tornado can give the illusion of merging with the dominant tornado as it moves behind its larger companion and becomes eclipsed from view. Unless the satellite tornado dissipates, it will usually quickly reappear from behind the bigger one.

Elephant trunk tornado

This tornado looks like an elephant's trunk (tube-like). It is mostly the same size from top to bottom (although the tornado may get somewhat wider near cloud base) and seems to come from the cloud in the same way that an elephant's trunk comes from the elephant's head. The tornado on the front cover of this book resembles an elephant's trunk.

Wedge Tornado

'Wedge' is informal storm observers' slang for a tornado that appears to be wider than the distance between the ground and the thunderstorm's cloud base. There is no scientific basis for the terminology, since many factors (moisture content of the air, intervening terrain, and soil and dust lifting) can affect what one sees.

Waterspout

Waterspouts can develop under several different conditions. Sometimes, a tornado can form over water from either a supercell or a non-supercell thunderstorm. The former is often referred to as a 'tornado over water' or a 'tornadic waterspout'. These are as potentially deadly and destructive as their land-formed counterparts, especially when, and if, they move ashore.

Waterspouts are often thin, semi-transparent tubes with a 'cloud' of spray at the water surface.

True waterspouts form from 'towering cumulus' clouds and sometimes even cumulus clouds. These have much weaker rotations and are correspondingly less dangerous. A true waterspout forms, in large part, due to 'superheated' water over shallow, coastal shoreline areas. Thus, this type of waterspout tends to form along the southeast and southern United States coasts.

This tornado shows its coiling character.

Landspout

These are much like non-supercell waterspouts on land. They are typically smaller and weaker than supercell-generated tornadoes. But since they are tornadoes by definition, they are capable of causing significant damage and harming people.

While the following are not really tornadoes, they exhibit many tornado-like characteristics. It is worthwhile noting their similarities and differences here.

Gustnado

Forming at the leading edge of a thunderstorm outflow, a gustnado is a small and usually weak whirlwind. It does not connect with any cloud-base rotation and is not considered to be a tornado. Because gustnadoes often have a spinning dust cloud at ground level, and are sometimes associated with threatening and turbulent clouds, they are frequently wrongly reported as tornadoes. Gustnadoes can do minor damage (e.g., break windows and tree limbs, overturn trash cans and toss lawn furniture).

Without the dust picked up by this tornado, you might not see it!

Dust Devil

Dust devils are small swirls that most often form over hot desert sands, asphalt parking lots, and other places that get 'superheated' in the daytime sun. As the air near the ground is warmed, it rises quickly upward, allowing air to rush in to take its place. Dust devils can form even in cloudless conditions. If there are clouds overhead, the dust devil is not connected to them. Winds in dust devils are usually less than 70 mph (110 kmph).

Snow Devil

These are short-lived swirls of snow that usually occur under windy conditions and also have no connection to any of the clouds above. Small variations in horizontal wind shear start them spinning; any type of rough terrain or treed area usually destroys them.

As important as these descriptive terms are, any tornado can change its characteristics moment by moment. An 'elephant trunk' tornado may shrink to a 'rope' as the storm moves over some rough terrain, only to reintensify as the storm moves onto more level ground. A tornado filled with debris or dust may lose its awesome appearance as it moves across an asphalt-covered shopping-center parking lot. Also, tornadoes often form as a series from the same parent supercell. The 3 May, 1999 outbreak in Oklahoma and the SuperOutbreak of Tornadoes (3-4 April, 1974) demonstrates this dramatically. When this happens, the older tornado usually weakens and a new tornado forms to its east or northeast. One reason this might happen is the occlusion process described earlier. Another might be that the older tornado is slowed by friction with the ground. Friction will slow the movement of the tornado, but not necessarily the movement of the parent cloud. When this happens, the parent cloud can separate from the older tornado and leave it behind to disintegrate. Then a new, more vertical tornado, may form. This break in the tornado's track may also help to account for reports that 'the tornado lifted as it approached my house and then touched down again a few blocks away'. In all likelihood, it may have actually been a different tornado.

With the right lighting conditions, it is possible to have a 'white tornado'.

Climatology

In the United States, peak tornado season occurs in the spring, when tornadoes are most frequent in the late afternoon and early evening. As the sun plays such a strong part in the development of tornadoes, it is not surprising that the tornado season develops across North America as the sun strengthens through the year. In late winter, the Gulf Coast region and Florida experience the most tornadoes. By middle spring, the southern part of 'tornado alley' becomes the hot spot. By mid-summer, southern Canada and the northern tier of the United States are under the greatest risk. Then when the sun heads south, the peak areas retrace their steps, albeit with a lower tornado frequency. The climatology is similar in other parts of the world. For example, Germany's peak tornado season (much like its high-latitude Canadian counterpart) is from June to August.

Spring is the peak tornado season because air mass contrasts are at their greatest, especially across 'tornado alley'. In some parts of the United States, 'cold-air' tornadoes occur not when the air near the ground is warm and humid, but rather, when the air aloft is very cold. This is often in fall, though sometimes in winter. Southern California's peak tornado season is in winter, which coincides with their rainy season.

Regardless of climatological information about tornadoes, these storms have been known to occur out of their season, at unexpected times of day, and outside of predictable areas. Tornadoes can occur along the 'dry line' or along cold fronts, and some even occur along warm fronts. Simply stated, if the weather conditions are right, twisters can happen any place, any time!

To better study the tornado climatology, the late Professor T. Theodore Fujita of the University of Chicago developed a scale to rate tornado strength by the type and amount of damage they cause. Fujita's Tornado Classification Scale, known simply as the F-scale, has become the base upon which the NWS and others worldwide evaluate storm damage. If you review the *Storm Data* publication or its online component, or the Storm Prediction Center's

There is no mistaking the debris cloud from this Pampa, Texas, tornado.

The power of the tornado is clearly evident in these photographs. In addition to snapping
and uprooting trees, flying debris often strips trees of their leaves and bark. The upper levels of homes
usually suffer the most damage because they are most exposed to wind and flying debris.

website classifications, you will find that they are coded by the highest F-scale damage reported for a particular storm. The intensity of a tornado may be categorized differently throughout its lifetime based on changes in storm intensity, ground effects, and the types of structures it damages. The F-scale is also used to classify non-tornadic storm events such as damage from downbursts.

There are some problems with the F-scale classification system. One of the most significant is that damage to structures must occur for the scale to be used effectively. An F-5 that occurs in a corn field may never be classified as an F-5 unless a knowledgeable person has observed the storm. In an attempt to address this problem, Dr G. Terence Meaden, of the UK, has developed another tornado scale, with increased wind speed resolution and an emphasis of including wind estimates from multiple sources (not only damage analysis). Both systems build on the Beaufort wind scale which is used primarily to estimate non-tornadic events.

Nobody knows the true wind speed of a

FUJITA'S F-SCALE

(F0) Gale tornado (40-72 mph / 64-116 kmph)   **Light damage.**
Some damage to chimneys; branches break off trees; shallow-rooted trees pushed over; sign boards damaged.

(F1) Moderate tornado (73-112 mph / 117-180 kmph)   **Moderate damage.**
The lower limit is the beginning of hurricane wind speed; roof damage; mobile homes knocked off foundations or overturned; moving autos pushed off the roads.

(F2) Significant tornado (113-157 mph / 182-253 kmph)   **Considerable damage.**
Roofs torn off frame houses; mobile homes demolished; boxcars pushed over; large trees snapped or uprooted; light-object missiles generated.

(F3) Severe tornado (158-206 mph / 254-332 kmph)   **Severe damage.**
Roofs and some walls torn off well-constructed houses; trains overturned; most trees in forest uprooted; heavy cars lifted off the ground and thrown.

(F4) Devastating tornado (207-260 mph / 333-418 kmph)   **Devastating damage.**
Well-constructed houses leveled; structures with weak foundations blown off some distance; cars thrown and large missiles generated.

(F5) Incredible tornado (261-318 mph / 420-512 kmph)   **Incredible damage.**
Strong frame houses lifted off foundations and carried considerable distance to disintegrate; automobile-sized missiles fly through the air; trees debarked; incredible phenomena will occur.

tornado on the ground. This is due to many shortfalls in our ability to observe, measure, and analyze the data we currently have. For example, Doppler radar measures wind speeds in tornadoes, but only by averaging motions over a volume. There are also significant effects due to the curvature of the Earth and changes in the size and shape of the radar beam with distance. Conventional wind instruments (e.g., wind vanes and anemometers) in or very close to a tornado are always either damaged or destroyed. Variances in wind damage due to building construction and/or condition often render wind estimates only to a single F-scale range. And, at times, even wind engineers and meteorologists experienced in storm damage surveys often disagree among themselves about a tornado's strength. Nonetheless, Fujita's F-scale provides a valuable tool for assessing storm damage, analyzing a storm's strength, and developing climatological storm data sets.

Because the F-scale relies so heavily on damage to classify wind speed, it is important to understand just how tornadoes damage and destroy things. Before more scientific studies were made, many people believed that tornadoes caused houses to explode. This was based on films and observations showing tornado damage from a distance. When a tornado passed by a house and debris suddenly went flying, it looked like an explosion.

In recent years, wind engineers have examined the complex set of forces that rip and tear houses apart. While the explosion theory described above is one possible way a house can be destroyed, there are many other events that create similar destructive results.

For example, suppose that wind damages something near your house. The wind then blows this debris into the side of your house and either makes a hole and/or breaks a window. Air flows through this opening, filling the house with excess air. This creates a higher pressure on the inside of the house that pushes on the other walls and the roof. Air flow over the roof creates a Bernoulli Effect which acts to lift the roof, much like moving air helps to lift an airplane wing. The roof may lift, even slightly, allowing air to get into the attic, further enhancing lift. Once the roof has been lifted away, the walls lose some structural support and are more susceptible to collapse. Since the tornado does all this quickly, debris is immediately thrown into the air. From a distance, the details can't be seen.

Winds in and near a tornado on the ground are slower than they are just above the ground due to friction. This means that objects and debris, once airborne, travel faster just above the ground. Therefore the tops of buildings and trees are more susceptible to damage, than the areas lower down.

These assessments have resulted in updated safety rules that recommend going to a small interior room on the lower level of a house when a tornado threatens. This places several layers of wall between you and the tornado and also gets you away from flying glass. A popular misconception is that you should open a window to try and equalize air pressure. This is unnecessary as the force of a tornado will easily blow windows in or out anyway. For most tornadoes, getting low down and far inside your house away from windows may be the best advice to help save your life.

Mobile homes are long and thin and are easily blown over if broad-sided by tornadic and other strong winds. Because they are open underneath and are relatively light, they are also susceptible to becoming airborne in high winds. Cars are not much different, although they give a false sense of security because you feel that you can outrun a tornado. Fatality statistics indicate that both mobile homes and cars are not the places to be in a tornado.

Finally, not all houses, even if they look the same, are constructed in the same way. Until the house is damaged or destroyed, homeowners may never know if their house has any

Tornadoes stronger than F1 can topple electric power pylons.

defects that might make it more likely to be damaged. Following Hurricane Andrew in south Florida in 1992, the roofs of many homes were blown off. These roofs were supposed to have been built to withstand winds of about 110 mph (177 kmph). After analyzing the damage, insurance adjusters, scientists, and government officials discovered that essential tie-down straps had not been installed in the roof area of many houses.

Similar unknown quantities hold true for damage to trees. Often, apparently large, sturdy trees are felled by high or tornadic winds. On closer inspection, one discovers that the tree may

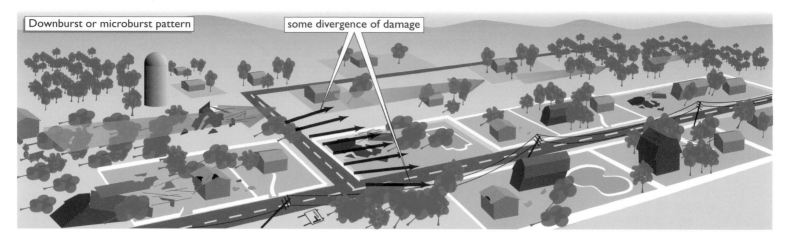

Downburst or microburst pattern

some divergence of damage

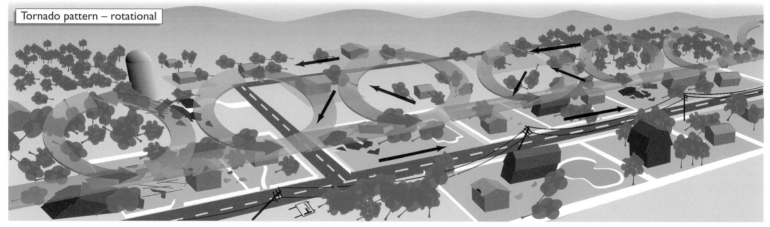

Tornado pattern – rotational

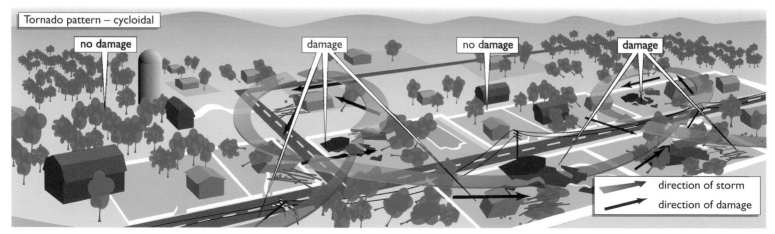

Tornado pattern – cycloidal

no damage

damage

no damage

damage

direction of storm

direction of damage

have been diseased or have suffered previous damage that weakened it. In urban areas, tree roots are more shallow because concrete and asphalt block water access to the roots, and the trees are therefore susceptible to wind damage.

The NWS has analyzed its tornado data records (built around Fujita's scale) and found many useful relationships. One of the most striking is that there is a direct relationship between a tornado's wind speed (F-scale number) and its lifetime. Simply by comparing weak (F0-F1), strong (F2-F3) and violent (F4-F5) tornadoes, it also becomes easy to see the relationship between tornado strength and fatalities. Fortunately, nearly all tornadoes fall into the weakest F-scale categories, with only 2 per cent considered to be violent. Not surprisingly, the corresponding number of deaths and injuries from weak to strong tornadoes is relatively small, but dramatically larger for the longer-lived and stronger F4 and F5 storms. It is important to note, however, that these are statistics. Significant variations can occur within categories. It is not unreasonable to suspect that even a weak tornado hitting a mobile home park can cause many fatalities.

Other interesting statistics involve tornado 'outbreak days' (days with more than ten tornadoes). Each year only a few 'outbreak days' occur. But some years have many. Typically outbreak days have the greatest number of casualties. According to NOAA's Storm Prediction Center, two-thirds of the 15 deadliest tornado years by state since 1950 involved outbreaks.

Geographical distribution is important, too. A map showing US tornado incidence was prepared in 1980 by Professor Fujita. This map shows many interesting facets of the tornado

Damage Patterns Caused by Downburst Winds and Tornadoes
Top: In downburst or microburst patterns, most trees and other damage occurs primarily in one direction. This is often referred to as 'straight-line' wind damage.
Middle: As a tornado moves across an area, almost anything in its path is subject to damage or destruction. Since the winds in a tornado are circular, debris patterns are usually scattered.
Bottom: Sometimes a tornado may rotate about a point outside of its center. When this happens, the path of the tornado may appear to 'wobble'. This creates 'gaps' and/or unusual events in the damage pattern even though the tornado may have appeared to move over the area.

Tornadoes: Strength vs Fatalities

There is a direct relationship between tornado strength and lifetime. While most tornadoes are weak and not deadly, the few violent tornadoes that occur each year are usually ranked as 'killers'.

	% of all tornadoes	% of tornado deaths	Lifetime
Weak Tornadoes (F0-F1) Winds up to 112 mph (180 kmph)	69 %	Less than 5%	1-10 + minutes
Strong Tornadoes (F2-F3) Winds 113-206 mph (182-331 kmph)	29 %	Nearly 30%	20 minutes or longer
Violent Tornadoes (F4-F5) Winds greater than 206 mph (332	2%	70%	Can exceed an hour

climatology. Most striking is the high incidence of tornadoes east of the Rocky Mountains, concentrated in tornado alley. About 90 per cent of tornado tracks run from southwest to northeast. This would be expected based on weather pattern analysis and where tornadoes occur within storm systems. In some locations (e.g., North Dakota and the northeast United States) the preferred track is from the northwest to the southeast.

There is a sharp boundary at the edge of the higher tornado frequency areas (e.g., along the Appalachian Mountains, along the front range of the Rocky Mountains, and near the Great Lakes). This suggests that terrain, drier air masses, and chilly lake water act to reduce tornado incidence.

The high frequency in Oklahoma and Kansas is likely linked to the efforts of storm spotters and chasers; since this map only considers tornadoes through 1978, the relationship would be even stronger today. In the western United States, reported tornado frequency is linked to population. If there is no one to observe the tornado, it may never be recorded. In recent years, as some urban areas have expanded, tornado incidence has increased. After Denver built its new airport and the city grew to the east, the number of tornadoes reported increased significantly.

The most tornadoes ever recorded in a 24-hour period occurred during the 'SuperOutbreak of Tornadoes' on April 3-4, 1974. This map, prepared by Professor Fujita documents the nearly 150 tornadoes that occurred in that Outbreak. At times, during the Outbreak, several tornadoes were on the ground at the same time. During this Outbreak, all tracks ran from southwest to northeast, as storms were carried along by high altitude, southwesterly, jet stream winds. Tornado tracks on this map show Fujita F-scale values and the approximate width of the damage path. Note that tornado intensity typically varies along each track.

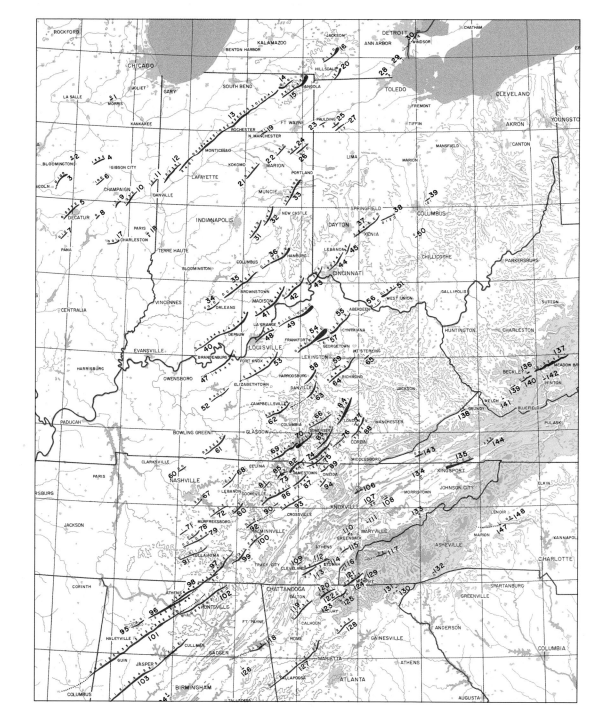

Significant and Unusual Tornado Events

NOAA's Storm Prediction Center (SPC) has created a list of the top 25 deadliest tornado events in US history. The list, dating back to 1840, can be found at http://www.spc.noaa.gov/archive/tornadoes/t-deadly.html.

The SuperOutbreak of Tornadoes on 3-4 April, 1974, with almost 150 tornadoes, remains the most prolific tornado event in recorded US history, and was responsible for some 315 deaths and more than 5000 injuries (see map on page 59). It began near St Louis about midday on 3 April, when a swath of twisters struck a 13-state area from Illinois to New York and from Michigan to Alabama. At least 36 tornadoes were classified as F4 or F5; 95 were F2 or greater. At the peak of the outbreak, at least 15 tornadoes were on the ground at the same time. Yet not one of the individual twisters during that outbreak was deadly enough to make the SPC list.

The tri-state tornado of 1925 was the deadliest twister in US history. It began in southeastern Missouri around 1 pm on 18 March and raced eastward at 60-70 mph (97-113 kmph) during its incredible more than 3-hour lifetime. This storm killed nearly 700 people and even wiped some small towns off the map. The 234 fatalities in Murphysboro is a record for a single community from such a disaster. Although F-scale ratings were not made at the time, this storm would have been classified an F-5 by meteorologists today.

All tornadoes on the complete SPC list occurred between March and June, and only three occurred in or east of the Appalachians. Since 1955, no single tornado has caused loss of life high enough to make this list. This provides some testimony to the value of the United States' tornado forecasting system.

FACT OR FICTION?
According to Roger Edwards at the SPC, tornadoes have been known to do some weird things. There are many tales about defeathered chickens, ponds that have been sucked dry, and skies

A tall, precipitation-laden thunderstorm creates an eerie nighttime look as a cone-shaped tornado passes.

that have 'rained frogs'. Unfortunately, it is sometimes impossible to separate fact from fiction. However, some things are known through scientific analysis and physical understanding.

For example, storm chasers and meteorologists who have surveyed storm damage have found many instances in which asphalt road pavement has been stripped. High-speed winds from strong to violent tornadoes sandblast the edges of the road surface with gravel and other small debris, literally eroding the edges and causing chunks to peel loose from the road base.

High winds can drive straws, large pieces of wood, and other objects into trees, buildings, fenceposts and cars. With a specially designed cannon, wind engineers at Texas Tech University (Lubbock) have fired boards and other objects at over 100 mph (160 kmph) into various types of construction materials, duplicating some of these kinds of effects. Sometimes, intense winds can bend a tree or other object, creating cracks in which debris (e.g., hay or straws) becomes lodged before the tree straightens and the crack tightens shut again. With careful study, it appears that most, if not all, of these bizarre damage effects can be explained by the laws of physics.

Tornadoes have also been known to transport objects for miles. There are numerous stories about tornadoes that have lofted (mainly light) debris many miles into the sky, which was then carried by middle- and upper-atmospheric winds for long distances. One of these events involved frog falls. In 1873 (Kansas City, Missouri) and again in 1883 (Cairo, Illinois) there were many reports of lots of frogs falling from the sky. There have been other reports about falling fish and even one about a 6 in by 8 in (15 cm by 20 cm) gopher turtle, entirely encased in ice, that fell with hail.

Not to be outdone by the animal world, people north of Keokuk, Iowa, found many unopened soda cans deposited by a tornado that had struck Moberly, Missouri, some 150 miles (240 km) away. The tornado had lifted these from a bottling plant and carried them to their eventual resting place.

Other recent tales involve infants picked up by tornadoes and deposited safely in trees. Some are found hanging by the straps of their baby clothing. Others, like 18-month-old Jonathan Waldick, of the Orlando, Florida area, have been found neatly wrapped in a mattress stuffed between tree branches. Large objects, like railway cars, tend to be blown over and

This rope-like twister shows that not every tornado fits the supercell model (page 21).

rolled, although they can be lifted and carried, at least for short distances. Again, as with damage reports, there are rational explanations for these unusual happenings.

Tornadoes are rare, but not uncommon, west of the continental divide. In July 1987, a tornado swept through Yellowstone National Park, near the divide itself, leaving a path of destruction up and down a 10,000 ft (3000 m) mountain. One year later, the tens of thousands of trees it destroyed became firewood for a raging series of forest fires that spread throughout the Park.

What are the chances of a tornado striking the same place twice in one day or striking the same city on the same date for three years in a row? Although these are pushing the limits of expected probability, they and other similar events have occurred. Here are just a few examples:

Codell, Kansas has been struck in three successive years (1916-1918), all on 20 May. During the 3-4 April, 1974 tornado outbreak, at least six towns were struck twice by tornadoes. During a September 1973 tornado outbreak in Kansas, a police car was struck by a tornado while it was driving through a community to warn residents of an approaching tornado. Several hours later, another twister struck the hospital the injured police officer had been taken to.

More than 100 tornadoes have touched down in Oklahoma City. If unusual and statistically rare events occur, so do events which, according to local legend shouldn't occur. Stories abound about places safe from tornadoes near forking rivers, mountains, and even hills. Yet, sooner or later, most of these are proven false. Residents of Topeka, Kansas, were supposed to be protected thanks to Burnetts Mound, an elevated region to the southwest of the city. According to local lore, tornadoes approaching the city would be deflected upward when they struck the mound and then return to Earth after passing by the city. That legend survived only until a tornado went up and then down the mound and passed right through the city in June 1966. Tornadoes raced across northern and western Pennsylvania on 31 May, 1985, caring little about the mountains in their way.

For many years, the urban legend was that tornadoes avoided major metropolitan areas because the wind flow within and around the city disrupted the tornado circulation. Scratch another legend. Between 1998 and 2000, the downtown areas of Nashville, Tennessee; Fort Worth, Texas; Salt Lake City, Utah; and Miami, Florida have all been struck by tornadoes.

Tornadoes are often easiest to spot when they are silhouetted against a light background.

Global Tornadoes

Although the United States has the greatest number of tornadoes, it is not alone in experiencing them. Many countries in mid-latitudes including Canada, the UK, France, Germany, Russia, South Africa, Australia, Bangladesh, and Japan also have a history of tornados. There have even been tornadoes reported in Trinidad.

According to Robin Maharaj, retired Chief Weather Officer on the island of Trinidad, '…the unique physical features of the island, its location close to Venezuela, and a nearly enclosed body of water, combine with strong heating of the ground and a sea breeze, to create strong thunderstorm development. Tornadoes, most commonly formed in the summer months at this low-latitude site, are generally weak and short-lived and are confined to flat terrain. There are waterspouts too, about 12 annually, during the same season, and favoring the Gulf of Paria's shallow water. They always seem to need a cumulonimbus cloud to form, making them different than many waterspouts in the United States.'

This global distribution suggests that the main ingredient for tornado formation (certain air mass clashes) are not the only factor to consider in assessing tornadic risk. Although some of these tornado occurrences involve waterspouts coming ashore, many do not. Unfortunately, documentation of tornadoes from around the world is far from comprehensive.

Reports about Canadian tornadoes are probably the most complete. This is probably because of Canada's proximity to tornado alley and the similarity between the Canadian and US severe weather forecasting services. The Edmonton, Alberta, tornado of 31 July, 1987 is probably the most well-known. Damage from this tornado was extensive and it caused 27 fatalities and about 250 injuries. The Windsor, Ontario, tornado, which killed nine people, was part of the 3-4 April, 1974 SuperOutbreak.

Tornadoes and waterspouts have been reported in many European countries. However, because of its longer historical record, we know of tornado occurrences there some 900 years ago. The earliest tornado known in the United Kingdom occurred in 1091. It was a very strong

A tornado, evident only as a cloud of dust, spins across the landscape near Ladakh, NE India.

tornado and it damaged or destroyed several churches in London. The earliest-known British (and also European) waterspouts occurred off the southern England coast in 1233. The largest tornado outbreak in Britain is also the largest tornado outbreak known anywhere in Europe. In November, 1981, 105 tornadoes were spawned by a cold front in slightly more than five hours. Excepting Derbyshire, every county in a triangular area from Gwynedd in Wales to Humberside and Essex was hit by at least one tornado, while Norfolk was hit by at least 13. Fortunately most of the tornadoes were short-lived and weak and no deaths occurred.

According to the Tornado and Storm Research Organisation (TORRO), tornadoes and waterspouts have caused considerable loss of life across Europe. In September 1551 or 1556 (the actual date is unclear), a waterspout struck the Grand Harbor at Valetta, Malta. It then moved ashore, causing substantial damage. A shipping armada, which had assembled there and was about to go into battle, was destroyed by the waterspout, killing at least 600 people.

In December 1851, two tornadoes apparently crossed the western tip of Sicily, Italy, killing over 500 people, while in June, 1984, a very strong tornado hit Belyanitsky, Ivanovo and Balino in western Russia, killing over 400 and injuring 213. In August 1845, a tornado struck Moneuil in France. This storm was more like a US tornado (stronger than its typical European counterparts). It caused extensive damage and killed hundreds. An F2 tornado struck Parma, Italy in July 2000, while another F2 struck Harrismith, South Africa, in November 1998.

There have been many documented tornadoes and waterspouts across Russia. Japan reports an average of about 20 tornadoes a year. Yet, it is Bangladesh where the strongest and most deadly twisters occur outside the United States. In May 1996, a series of tornadoes struck the districts of Jamalpur and Tangail in Bangladesh, killing more than 600 people. Perhaps the deadliest single tornado in the world occurred in Manikganj, Bangladesh, on 29 April 1989. Approximately 1300 people died, 12,000 were injured, and some 80,000 were made homeless. This toll is likely linked to a weak severe-weather warning system, a high density of people, and less well-constructed buildings.

Waterspouts have been reported globally, too. They have been sighted in the western Caribbean Sea, in the Baltic and Black Seas, in the South China Sea, and in the Gulf of Finland. In 1775, Captain Cook saw six waterspouts simultaneously near the coast of New Zealand.

Tornadic waterspout (elephant trunk atop and cone-shaped beneath) travels across the Baltic Sea near Gotland Island, Sweden. The spray of water shows that tornadic circulation has reached the water surface. Otherwise, this might have been classified incorrectly as a funnel cloud.

Glossary

air mass - a large body of air with similar conditions of temperature and humidity.

back-sheared anvil - a thunderstorm anvil which spreads upwind, against the wind flow aloft.

Bernoulli effect - the process by which pressure is lowered as a fluid moves faster.

cumulus clouds - vertically developing clouds characterized by relatively flat bases and dome-shaped tops.

cumulonimbus - a tall cumulus cloud with a flattened, often fibrous, cirrus top. Also referred to as a 'thunderhead'.

derecho - a widespread, fast-moving, and destructive downburst event associated with thunderstorms.

dew point - a measure of atmospheric water vapor content; the temperature to which air must be cooled, at constant pressure and moisture content, in order for condensation to occur.

Doppler radar - a radar system that measures both standard precipitation reflectivity or 'echoes' and the instantaneous component of wind motion toward or away from the radar.

downburst - a strong downdraft and outflow of straight-line winds initiated by a thunderstorm; often produces a star-shaped or elongated damage pattern.

downdraft - current of air with marked downward vertical motion within a cumulus-type cloud.

dry line - a boundary separating moist and dry air masses, typically lying north-south across the western part of 'tornado alley'.

funnel cloud - a rotating column of air that is not in contact with the ground; usually seen as a cloud-like funnel attached to a thunderstorm cloud.

Fujita scale - a scale devised by Dr Theodore Fujita from the University of Chicago and used to classify the strength of a tornado based on an assessment of damage.

hook echo - a pendant or hook on the right rear edge of a radar echo that often identifies a mesocyclone on a standard radar display.

overshooting top - a dome-like protrusion above a thunderstorm anvil, representing a very strong updraft; if large and persistent, indicates a high potential for severe weather.

mammatus clouds - rounded, smooth, sack-like protrusions hanging from the underside of a thunderstorm anvil.

mesocyclone - a region of rotation, typically 2-6 miles (3-10 km) in diameter, that is often found in the right rear flank of a supercell thunderstorm.

mesoscale convective system (MCS) - a cluster of thunderstorms that does not satisfy the size, shape, or duration criteria of an MCC.

mesoscale convective complex (MCC) - large, generally round or oval-shaped area of thunderstorms. Based on satellite image criteria, an MCS is typically at least the size of Ohio and lasts at least 6 hours.

roll cloud - a low, horizontal tube-shaped cloud most often associated with a thunderstorm gust front; cloud appears to be 'rolling' about a horizontal axis and is detached from the thunderstorm cloud.

shelf cloud - a low, horizontal wedge-shaped thunderstorm accessory cloud; this cloud has rising cloud motion at its leading edge, while the underside often appears turbulent, boiling, and wind-torn. It is accompanied by gusty, straight-line winds and is followed by precipitation.

squall line - a line or narrow band of thunderstorms; the line, usually along and/or ahead of a cold front, may be several hundred miles long.

supercell - a thunderstorm, with a persistent rotating updraft, which often produces severe weather and tornadoes.

tornado - a violently rotating column of air in contact with the ground, attached to a cumulonimbus cloud, and nearly always observable as a funnel-shaped cloud.

tornado alley - a region of the Central Plains which includes Nebraska, Kansas, Oklahoma, and parts of north Texas in which the number of reported tornadoes in the US is the highest.

tornado vortex signature (TVS) - a region on a Doppler radar screen that shows a high degree of rapidly changing cyclonic wind speeds within a small region.

updraft - current of air with marked upward vertical motion within a cumulus-type cloud.

vorticity - a measure of the local rotation or spin around a vertical axis in a fluid flow.

wall cloud - a localized, persistent, sometimes rotating, often abrupt lowering of the base of a supercell thunderstorm cloud. It can be a fraction of a mile to up to nearly five miles (8 km) in diameter, and normally is found on the south or southwest (inflow) side of the thunderstorm.

warning - a word used by local NWS offices indicating that a particular weather hazard is either imminent or has been reported.

watch - a word used by the NWS to indicate that a particular hazard is possible, i.e., that conditions are more favorable than usual for its occurrence.

wave cyclone - a low-pressure system that forms in middle- or high-latitudes and has associated warm and cold fronts attached to it.

windshear - the variation in wind speed (speed shear) and/or direction (directional shear) over a short distance. It can involve many different situations, but is commonly applied to significant changes in wind speed and/or direction that contribute to airplane crashes.

Index

*Entries in **bold** indicate pictures*

Biographical Note

H Michael Mogil is a professional meteorologist with degrees from Florida State University. He worked for NOAA as a forecaster, researcher, trainer and program manager for nearly 30 years before retiring. Since 1979, he has operated his own educational services company - How The Weatherworks.
He has written scores of articles and has co-authored several books. Mike and his wife Barbara have collaborated on several award-winning weather products all of which are widely used in schools across the nation. The National Weather Association has recognized him for his 'outstanding efforts in weather education.' He lives and works in Rockville, Maryland.

Recommended Reading

Bluestein, H B *Tornado Alley - Monster Storms of the Great Plains* Oxford University Press, 1999

Eagleman, J R *Severe and Unusual Weather* Trimedia Publishing Company, 1990

Ludlum, D M *Early American Tornadoes: 1586-1870* American Meteorological Society, 1970

Rosenfeld, J *Inside The World's Deadliest Hurricanes, Tornadoes, and Blizzards* Plenum Publishing, 1999

Web Links

NOAA's National Climatic Data Center
http://www.ncdc.noaa.gov/ol/climate/severeweather/tornadoes.html
NOAA's Severe Storm Laboratory
http://www.nssl.noaa.gov/
NOAA Southern Region Headquarters
http://www.srh.noaa.gov/oun/skywarn/spotterguide.html
NOAA's Storm Prediction Center
http://www.spc.noaa.gov
NOAA Tornado Preparedness Guide
http://www.nws.noaa.gov/om/tornado.htm
StormTrack
http://www.stormtrack.org
Tornado and Storm Research Organisation
http://www.torro.org.uk